Rider, Rider

Corrine Andros

BookLeaf
Publishing

India | USA | UK

Presentation by *BookLeaf Publishing*

Web: www.bookleafpub.com

E-mail: info@bookleafpub.com

ISBN: 9789357447263

First edition 2022

DEDICATION

Rider, Rider is dedicated to all the jockeys.

ACKNOWLEDGEMENT

Thank you to my mom for always believing in me and all the powerful women in my family who never gave up on themselves or us.

Rider, Rider

Rider, Rider
Heart of Fire
Let them burn in your desire
Take your passion and shove it down their
throats
Sing your song, don't miss a note

One day, they are going to know.

Jockey

Don't tell me you know the cost of this life until you've paid for yourself in full.

Imagine

There is a place in my mind where you planted
trees and gave them voices
Where the flowers dance
And the willow sways, whispering it's stories
I can't believe this is the result for my choices
I just hope the warmth stays

Horse

When the ground gave way to flame
You carried me
When I felt I had no heart
You gave me yours

Though my body may grow stiff
And my bones ache from the injuries of this
craft
With you, I still fly

Wrongs are forgiven
Everyday a lesson learned
Or a heart is healed when soft hands connect
with a soft mouth

No one will know the sacrifice
No one will feel the pain or the scars they can't
see

But you know
And I see you
I see me through your eyes.

Unconditional

I love in the way of a gentle breeze
Caressing your hair as I gently brush by
I love you as strong as the seven seas
Endless and Powerful
I'll love you as long as the sun lives
Until the very last of life
I love you as deep as the starry black skies
Infinite, unfathomable.

Forever, Unconditional.

Nirvana

Your thoughts come to mind as if they are my
own
Negotiation
Decisions
Reaching
Breathing
Extending
We call each other into transcendence
A divine performance is revealed
As two individuals become one

For all the escapes there are in this world
You are my favourite
You are the keeper of the keys to Nirvana
And you are my keeper
I give you my heart and soul
Over and over and over...

Phoenix

My chest aches with gratitude
Replacing the scars
Through the tears
In my heart grow roses
From the holes in my back shine stars
Little did you realize
You can light up the ground around me
From the ash I will rise

I no longer speak your language
I can't recognize your tongue
Continuing my ascension
One day it will be as if your song were never
sung.

Healing

I sit with the silence
A welcome blanket
The voice of an old friend
What used to terrify me doesn't anymore
With silence I find a reflection of myself
An opportunity for healing and growth
Don't turn away from the silence
Face yourself
Welcome and feel it
Acknowledge and let go
Breathe.

Creators

We exist as one but perceive a separation
Somehow lies were created
False Teachings of stolen love letters
Brainwashed to forget our origin

Can't you feel it when you feel love
Can't you see the beauty you create
Right infront of our eyes is the truth
Yet we remain blind
To our eternity
To our light
Afraid of or enchanted by our own darkness

Acceptance of yourself begins with you
Empathize with yourself
Understand and love yourself
It isn't always easy
But it is a choice
It is beautifully painful
As any rebirth should be.

Strength

If only you knew the truth

My heart screams out into the quiet
My spirit is relentless
Even when every other piece of me begs to stop
My heart cries it can't take anymore
And then it does
On the edge of shattering
Though it never will
I swallow the pain the way a dragon might
swallow fire
It belongs to me and not I to it
I turn it into my most powerful weapon
Smiling as the flames lick behind my teeth
Sweet with passion and love.

I may stumble but I can not stop
Failure is only found in giving up
Real hell is regret
Where I refuse to live
Forward I go.

Successful

I mark myself
Not by my accomplishments
Not by my failures
But by my refusal to give up
I know my strength is bottomless
This is my success

Winner's Circle

Here is that feeling of relief
A reward for the hard work and years of
perseverance
Through injury, mental battles, against the odds
& just for being a woman
Winning comes at a price
Just putting your feet in those pedals comes at a
higher cost than most could imagine
A moment of glory
For endless blood, sweat, tears and a repeatedly
broken heart
Quitting doesn't exist if you want to call yourself
by the title
You either are or you never were.

New Lenses

I never learned to love the world until I saw it from the backs of horses.

Rise

Shed away the darkness
Like a snake sheds its skin
Shake away the last drops of pain from your
fingertips
And look back up over that summit
Angels were never made to be broken
Love can not fail.

Persevere

I refuse to be another story of one who could
have but didn't make it.

Destiny

I've met a wicked beautiful thing
She goes by destiny
Sometimes sweetness she does sing
Sometimes she brings out the worst in me
She holds the secret to all my glory
And opens the door for all my sorrow
Oh Destiny
I'll see her in every tomorrow.

Racehorses

Some horses just hold your heart the way the sky
holds the stars
Though you may not see them all the time
They keep a piece of you with them
And give a piece of themselves in return
They will shine somewhere in your heart and
soul forever.

Teachers

One day when you hear me speak
You'll remember what I used to say
Perhaps I'll have the honor of being the voice in
the back of your mind
The one that teaches you a lesson you'll never
forget

The habit is developed by the repetition of the
voices in my head
The voices of many riders who laid down a path
before me
Who cared enough to show me their vision
The ones who cheered so loud
I can still feel the reverberations in my heart

I hope that I can be that rider
One day when I'm looking back
Who gave all I had to give to the ones still
fighting

This sport will never be easy
But if it were it wouldn't do
We all have something iron inside us
Something that gives us the push to keep going
I couldn't stop if I wanted to
I have accepted this.

Warrior

I am unafraid
To reach into my depths
And pull the darkest of my darkness
I am unafraid to face me and the world too
In all my scars and all my pain
For all the mistakes and mismanaged time
I became what I am
Or returned to who I should have always been

The mountains are etched slowly under pressure
By the wind and by the sea
Formed are the greatest peaks
I will rise
As a phoenix always has
From the ashes of what I used to be
Different in so many ways
Yet still me

I am worthy
I am loved
Even if I fail
Even if I never reach what I set out to do
What I give my life for

I love me

For I have seen the unimaginable
And survived
I fought as a warrior does
To be where and who I am
Thankful.

Ugly

How ugly is a rock
When the tides changed a million times to create
it
When a billion waves crashed down upon it
And it withstood
Only becoming more polished and beautiful
The rock never ceased to exist
Only reformed

And the waves never stopped crashing
Earth never stopped turning
The moon rose and gave way to the sun
Ever reaching
Too many lives and deaths have passed
And yet the rock remains
From what was once a mountain
Or the heart of it all

How could it be ugly
A creation in itself
Weathered by what we know as time
Withstanding through all creation
Perfection in imperfection

Forever breaking down
Forever growing

My Son

You think you know what unconditional is
and then you hold it in your arms
Gravity shifts and the whole world changes
Everything that didn't make sense doesn't matter
anymore
It all makes sense now with you
Only you know how long I waited to love you...